STRIP IT

Dek Messecar

Series Consultant Editor: Bob Tattersall

CONTENTS

COLLINS

Introduction

This book tells you, clearly and simply, how to strip and re-finish furniture, floors and woodwork in your home. If you have a particular project in mind, you will find all the necessary information—materials and tools needed, tips, etc.—on a few pages in the appropriate section. If you're wondering whether it would be a good idea to introduce the natural wood look into your home, there are plenty of illustrations to set you thinking and to show what can be achieved.

Why strip? It is the warm, natural look of wood that has made stripping popular, but there are practical advantages too! Modern wood finishes are easy to care for; if they get the odd knock, it doesn't show as with painted surfaces. At most, all a natural finish needs is an occasional coat of wax—much easier than re-painting—and it is just as easy to keep clean as paint. Wood looks better and more comfortable with normal wear and improves with age.

A natural wood finish is certainly the least expensive flooring and one of the best-looking. Stripping is cheap, although you have to be prepared to devote a lot of time to it, and you have the satisfaction of knowing that the results are uniquely yours.

What to strip. Floors are a most rewarding project because of the impact a new floor has on a room. It doesn't matter whether the old floor is parquet or pine boards, a polished wooden floor has a character distinct from any other.

Cupboards, shelves and fireplaces in older houses are often original and of good workmanship. By stripping, you completely transform them, often drawing attention to features that would otherwise not be noticed.

Doors, window frames and other woodwork are obvious candidates for stripping. Of course, stripping all the woodwork in a room is an enormous undertaking, but if you tackle just parts of it—say a particular feature—you can draw attention to it and often tie the room and furniture together visually.

Finally, any wooden furniture can be

Above: *Stripping one feature of the woodwork can be as effective as stripping all of it.*

Right: *The stripped softwood floor matches the table top, and continuing the same floor through the next room creates a feeling of space.*

dramatically changed by stripping. By giving different pieces the same finish, you can combine the most unlikely periods and styles.

You can often find reasonably priced furniture in junk shops and at auction sales, but don't forget to look around your home and in your own attic first.

After stripping. You can change the colour of the wood by bleaching or staining it accordingly. Then you must give the surface protection from dirt and the drying effect of air. It is usual to seal the wood with a matt polyurethane sealer, followed by several coats of wax. For very hard wear, a surface film of polyurethane varnish or urea-formaldehyde is best. However, you will find details of more traditional finishes, and where to use them, later in the book.

FURNITURE AND WOODWORK

The most important point is to start small! If you strip and re-finish a small box or one chair, you will be in a position to know which method of stripping suits you, and how far your patience and enthusiasm will take you. As with all DIY projects, the time necessary to complete a job will probably be more than you imagine, so build your skill and confidence with care.

There are three main categories of furniture and woodwork: softwood, solid hardwood, and veneered hardwood.

Softwood. 'Country' furniture, as it is sometimes called, was usually made of pine or other softwood and was nearly always meant to be painted. This is why the pine chests and dressers, so popular today in stripped form, often have joints that can be seen.

Included in this category is nearly all the woodwork or joinery in houses, both old and new. Cupboards, skirtings, window-frames, doors, shutters, panelling, etc. are usually softwood.

Hardwood. Solid hardwoods such as mahogany, oak, walnut or beech have traditionally been considered superior to softwoods and worthy of a polished finish. This requires a more sophisticated construction to hide the joints. Most chairs are made of hardwood because of its strength and durability. A well-made piece of hardwood furniture will last indefinitely, given reasonable conditions and occasional attention. This is true for hardwood household joinery, although it is rarely found. You could find a mahogany mantelpiece or bannister under layers of paint.

Small boxes such as these can sometimes be found in junk shops, and make an ideal project for the beginner.

A plate glass screen replaces an unwanted door without lessening the natural effect of the woodwork.

Far right *Carefully stripped and renovated, this old larder cupboard now has pride of place in an all-white living room. It has been waxed to achieve a pleasing matt finish.*

Veneer. This is a thin layer of decorative wood which is glued to solid wood beneath. The technique of veneering allows you to have furniture with the outward appearance of beautiful woods, while the carcase of the piece is made from a timber that is stronger, more stable, and better suited for construction. Generally speaking, veneered furniture is the most delicate of the three types, and the most difficult to repair.

Marquetry (inlay) is a form of veneering that consists of a pattern of pieces of veneer inlaid in the surface of solid wood or veneer. It isn't normal to find veneer on old woodwork, but test in an inconspicuous place.

Having chosen the piece you intend stripping, you may first want to identify the type of wood from which it is made. Use the identification guide on pages 6–7. If the furniture has a natural finish, you will be able to see at a glance, but if it is painted look carefully for a bit of bare wood to see what is underneath. A gentle scrape with a penknife in an inconspicuous spot may help you to see what colour the wood will be when stripped.

Look for signs of woodworm (borer). This must be treated with a proprietary product as soon as possible to prevent it from spreading. Check also for any repairs that may be needed. Inspect painted articles for signs of badly-done repairs that may have been covered deliberately. The repairs described on the following pages will give you an idea of the defects to watch out for, and enable you to decide what you feel you can tackle.

Types of Wood

Here are illustrations of some of the most common woods found in furniture, floors, and woodwork in Europe and North America. Practices vary in different parts of the world according to availability and price, but the same general rules apply.

Softwoods have always been the least expensive wood for all household joinery. Included in this category are whitewood, spruce, Douglas fir or Oregon, European redwood, hemlock, and several species of pine, such as Eastern and Western white

European Whitewood – is a softwood of the type that is popularly called 'pine'. It is used for all types of woodwork, furniture, and floorboards.

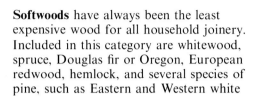

American White Oak – has similar properties to European oak and has been very popular for woodstrip and woodblock floors because of its colour and durability. One property of oak is that ferrous metals (iron or steel nails and screws) can discolour it. Always use brass or copper fixings.

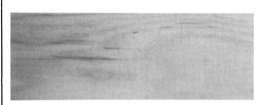

Douglas Fir – is similar to European Whitewood and is grown in North America, New Zealand and Europe.

Ash – is especially good for frame making due to its toughness.

European Oak – is a very hard and durable wood that has long been used for furniture, floors, and woodwork of every type. Although usually used in solid construction, it is sometimes found as veneer. It is also very weather resistant when used outside.

Beech – is a fine textured and resilient wood that is popular for chairs, worktops, and desks, etc.

pine (North America), pitch pine, Scots pine, parana pine, and radiata pine (Australia and New Zealand). These are all fine textured, close-grained woods and don't need to have their grain filled to get a smooth finish on them.

Hardwoods are found either in solid construction or used as veneer. Although not all hardwoods are actually harder than softwoods (balsa wood is a hardwood!) the common hardwoods are generally more resistant to denting and scratching.

Western Red Cedar – is a softwood and is used for exterior claddings and joinery because of its resistance to weather. As with oak, you should use non-ferrous nails and screws.

Walnut – is most distinctive as veneer as it can have a very wild and decorative grain (burr walnut), but is also used for legs and frames in solid form. Usually finished medium brown.

Mahogany – is a beautiful wood that has long been a favourite with cabinet makers and joiners for its colour and also because of the smooth finish it gives.

Rosewood – is usually a veneer with some solid pieces although it has sometimes been used to make solid tables or underframes.

Yew – is most often seen as a veneer. Although it is technically a softwood, it is hard and durable.

Teak – is the most durable wood known. It contains a natural oil that resists parasites and fungi. It is most suited to an oil finish. In fact, to apply any seal or varnish, it is necessary to scrub the natural oil off the surface with white spirit.

Damage and Repairs

There are many simple repairs you may have to make. The most common faults are loose joints, splits and warping. Dealing with these usually involves the use of glue and you must take care not to get this on to the bare surface of the wood. In particular, make sure no glue is rubbed into the grain, for it can show through later as a patch under the finish. Carrying out these repairs *before* you strip the wood helps to protect it from the glue and makes it possible to wipe off the excess while it is still wet.

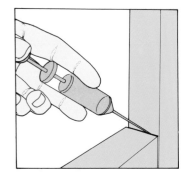

Loose joints

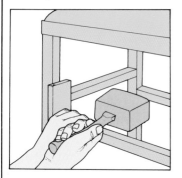

To dismantle a joint, hold one part of it firmly and tap the other part with a mallet. Use a block of wood to protect the piece you are striking. Do not bend the joint too far out of alignment or you may break it.

The original hide glue used in furniture making softens when warmed and moistened. For a stubborn joint, try placing a damp cloth over it and warming it gently with a domestic iron.

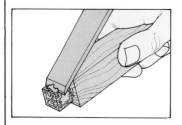

Scrape the old glue off the parts of the joint.

Any proprietary wood glue will do when you come to re-make the joint, but badly fitting, wobbly joints need a gap-filling (non-shrinking) glue to help keep them tight. A glue that is transparent when set is an advantage, and of course you should follow the manufacturers' instructions.

Modern glues are almost impossible to remove once set, so be sure to get the alignment of the joint right the first time. You won't be able to dismantle it again. A 'dry run', re-assembling the parts without glue, should ensure all goes smoothly, although it may be a little more difficult to slide the parts together once the glue has been applied.

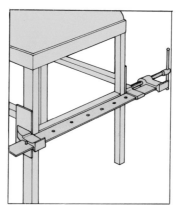

Clamp the parts together until the glue has set.

If the loose joint cannot be taken apart, perhaps because it would mean dismantling many other joints, try opening it as much as possible and working a gap-filling glue as far into it as you can. Sometimes a large hypodermic syringe can be useful for this. Be sure to clamp the parts securely until the glue has set.

Masking tape applied along the line where the parts meet will keep the squeezed-out glue from marring the surface. Once the joint is clamped, and the excess glue squeezed out, peel off the tape. Don't wait until the glue hardens.

Splits

Legs and posts should have glue thoroughly worked into any splits, and then be clamped tightly.

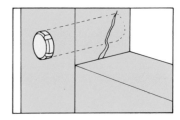

A dowel inserted through the split will greatly increase the strength of the repair, but be sure to make the hole where it won't be seen.

Panels split when the wood shrinks (wood shrinks in width, not in length). The most likely place is where two pieces are joined edge to edge. In such cases the edges are straight and the gap fairly constant.

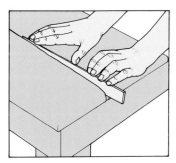

The best remedy is to shape a thin piece of matching wood to fill the gap, glue and tap it into position. This piece should be slightly wedge-shaped so that it fits tighter as it is pushed deeper into the split, and it should stand proud of the surface. The excess can be pared with a chisel or planed once the glue has set, taking care not to damage the surrounding wood. Finally, finish with fine abrasive paper wrapped around a block to leave the repair smooth.

Warping

Warped wood can sometimes be straightened, but there is no guarantee of success. Wood shrinks and swells in width and thickness according to its moisture content, but different sides of the same piece shrink or swell to a greater or lesser extent. The result is bending

and twisting of the wood.

None of these remedies should be tried until the wood has had time (several weeks) to become accustomed to the conditions in which it will live—and then they should be used gently. Drastic measures are to be avoided, and they probably won't produce a lasting cure anyway.

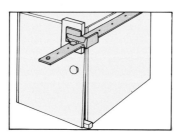

If cupboard doors are twisted, try clamping them closed with a small block of wood holding one corner slightly open, twisting the door in the opposite direction to the warp. So, if the top corner does not close properly, clamp it closed and place the block to prevent the bottom corner closing. Inspect the door after a few days to see whether the remedy is working. If not, leave it clamped for longer.

For solid (i.e. not veneered) panels or table tops that are warped, try slightly moistening the concave side with a damp cloth and a warm iron. On no account should moisture be used on veneer as it could loosen it or, worse, swell it.

Sometimes panels are finished on one side only. This means that the unfinished side will respond much more quickly to changes in humidity so strip and leave to dry before trying to straighten.

Other problems

Blisters in veneer (or edges that have lifted) are simple to repair.

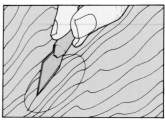

Use a sharp knife and a straight edge to cut through the blister in one stroke, starting just before the blister and continuing, along the grain, just past it. With a penknife, gently scrape out any debris under the veneer and work glue underneath as far as possible.

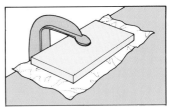

Use either a clamp or a heavy weight to press a flat piece of wood firmly on top of the repair. Place a sheet of polythene between the repair and the piece of wood to prevent them sticking together. Leave for 24 hours and then rub down with fine abrasive paper wrapped around a block, being very careful to rub with the grain and not to sand through the veneer.

Knots. Pine furniture may contain knots that have become loose. Glue back into position exactly level with the surface as they are very hard to smooth down afterwards.

Stripping Paint and Varnish

There are several methods of removing paint and varnish from wood. In general it is best to adopt the least drastic method that will be effective. For instance, it is better to use a chemical stripper that can be cleaned off with white spirit rather than water, since it is never a good idea to soak wood with water. However, if the article is so large that you would have to use vast quantities of liquid, or if you elect to use the newer forms of chemical stripper such as the paste or blanket methods then it will have to be water. This choice applies to solid wood—never use water on veneered surfaces!

Whichever method you select, remember to protect everything except whatever you're stripping. This includes your hands and clothes. Paint stripper burns skin and should be immediately washed off with cold water if contacted. Make sure you work in a well ventilated area because the fumes from the stripper can be overpowering. To guard against drips and splashes, place the article (if it's movable) on many layers of newspapers or put newspapers all around it. You should remove metal fittings.

The other point to remember is to proceed slowly on one area or surface at a time. There is nothing more frustrating than rushing from one patch to another, never quite finishing properly.

Tools and materials: Enough stripper for the area you are working on (see manufacturers' instructions); various metal scraping knives; coarse wire wool; an old paint brush; a metal container (not plastic) to scrape the paint into; lots of newspapers; rubber gloves; white spirit; clean rags; a container of clean water in case of accidents; scrubbing brush; trowel (for paste method); plastic spatula (for blanket method); thick working gloves (for blowtorch or hot air methods).

Liquid and jellied chemical strippers

Choose one that is soluble in both water and white spirit to give you the choice when cleaning it off. Wipe the surface to be stripped with white spirit to remove any wax.

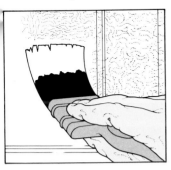

Brush the stripper on quite thickly and allow it to remain until the paint begins to crinkle. If there are many layers of paint, it will take some time for the stripper to penetrate.

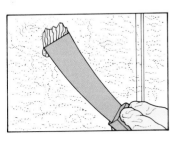

Push some of the paint aside with a scraper to see if the bare wood has been reached. If you can see the wood, or if the stripper seems to have stopped working, gently scrape off the mixture of paint and stripper into the metal container. Re-apply stripper to areas of paint that remain—don't be tempted to dig at stubborn areas with the scraper as you will damage the wood.

When all the surface layers of paint are gone, dip a piece of wire wool in stripper and rub the surface with it to remove the last traces. As each piece of wire wool becomes clogged with paint, put it into the container with the scrapings and start another piece.

When all the paint or varnish is removed, the surface must be cleaned thoroughly to remove all traces of the stripper which would otherwise dissolve the new finish. If you are using water, a scrubbing brush is useful for getting into grooves and corners. Remember that water will raise the grain of the wood and mean more sanding smooth later. [Don't use water on veneer.] The alternative to water is white spirit applied with wire wool and then with a cloth. Keep cleaning until you are certain all trace of the stripper is gone.

A new liquid stripper is becoming available (in some markets) that doesn't need to be washed, just peeled off.

Metal fittings, e.g. handles, hinges, etc., that you have removed can be stripped by leaving them in a glass jar of liquid stripper. When the paint has dissolved, rinse well and allow to dry.

Paste strippers

These are less messy than the liquids, especially on vertical and overhead surfaces. There are two types, both applied as a paste, but one combines with the paint and peels off with it. It is sometimes possible to re-use the paste, provided it has been kept moist. Their main disadvantage is that they must

be washed off with water and so can not be used on veneer. There can also be a tendency for paste strippers to darken wood, though this can be remedied by using a colour restorer.

First wipe the work with white spirit to remove any wax.

Trowel on the paste at least 3mm thick, working it well into crevices and corners and making sure there are no air bubbles under it. The paste must be kept moist while it works, so cover it with a sheet of polythene or give it an occasional spray of water. It may take from fifteen minutes to several hours for every layer of paint to be penetrated, so check for bare wood periodically by lifting a small area of the paste.

When you think it's ready, gently lift the paste and paint

11

(they will come off in pieces) or, if you're using the peelable type, peel the layer of paint and stripper away from the wood and place in the container. Keep re-applying moist paste as necessary to remove all the paint. To clean off, use water and a scrubbing brush or wire wool until you are certain all trace of the stripper is gone. Use plenty of clean water for a final rinse and allow to dry thoroughly.

Blanket method

This is a chemical stripping method that uses a paste on which you place a special fibrous blanket. This makes it possible to peel the blanket off together with the old paint. It is very useful for complex shapes and hard-to-reach places and is the least messy stripper to use. Against it, however, is the fact that it takes longer to work than the others and must be cleaned off afterwards with water; so it shouldn't be used on veneer or particularly good pieces of furniture.

Mix the powder with water according to the instructions, stir, and leave to stand for ten minutes.

Apply a thick layer of paste over an area that can be covered with the blanket (if

necessary, cut the blanket to suit the area you're stripping). Make sure the paste is worked well into corners, grooves, etc. Wet the blanket in soapy water, wring out, and apply it to the pasted surface (it should cling without being supported).

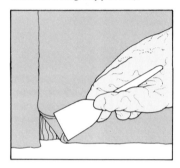

Leave it for two hours and then, using the plastic spatula, peel back a small part of the blanket to see if bare wood is showing underneath. If it isn't, cover again with the blanket and leave for another hour. Keep testing occasionally until every layer of paint is penetrated, showing the wood beneath.

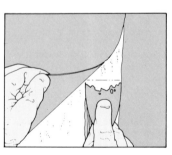

Wearing the gloves, peel the blanket away with one hand and lift off the paint with the spatula, keeping paste, paint and blanket together as much as possible. Wash the blanket well in hot soapy water, after

removing as much of the paint residue as you can. Leave the blanket in the water, ready for the next use. Re-apply fresh paste to any areas of paint remaining, using the blanket only if it seems it will be necessary to leave it some hours.

When all the paint is gone, remove any paste from the wood by scrubbing with a solution of warm water and a little vinegar. Sponge off, using single strokes and a warm water and vinegar solution. Finally, wipe all the wood with a cloth and neat vinegar. Allow to dry.

Blowtorches

Modern blowtorches work off liquid gas. They soften paint effectively and inexpensively, but great care must be taken not to scorch the wood, as burns can be difficult to remove. Do not use near glass, such as windows. Work with the grain, and try not to dig into the surface.

The paint softens when hot, but will re-harden as it cools off. So scrape off the paint as soon as it is ready. Wear a thick glove on the hand holding the scraper, and take care not to drop warm scrapings on bare skin. Put out any fire, no matter how small,

Stripping Clear Finishes

that you may cause. Burn off until you reach the last layer of paint, then finish with a chemical stripper and steel wool.

Hot air guns

These direct a stream of hot air at the paint to soften it. They do not work quite so quickly as a blowlamp, but they do not scorch, do not set the paint alight, and, with the correct nozzle, can be used near glass.

Caustic dipping

A commercial process, not suitable for do-it-yourself use. It should only be considered as a last resort as there can be warping and loosening of joints. Caustic removes all the natural oils from wood and leaves it looking bleached out and slightly greyish. It is necessary to neutralise the caustic after dipping and some companies do this but, if there is any doubt, rinse the article with a solution of vinegar and water and finally with clean water. When dry, some of the colour can be put back with a proprietary colour restorer.

Tips

After caustic dipping, hose down large articles in the garden or yard.

Don't use water on veneer.

Don't dig at stubborn areas with a scraper—you'll damage the wood. Apply more stripper.

First you must find out what finish you are trying to remove. Begin by rubbing an area with a cloth dipped in white spirit to dissolve any wax on the surface. Keep rubbing until the cloth remains clean. If you seem to be getting down to bare wood and still removing something, then you are dealing with a *wax* or *oil finish*.

If the cloth and white spirit stop affecting the finish on your test area, dab on some methylated spirit and see if the surface becomes tacky. If it does then the finish is *French polish* (or some other *shellac-based polish*).

If your test area was not affected by methylated spirits, the finish is either *varnish* or *cellulose lacquer*.

Wax or Oil Finish: Scrub the wood with white spirit and fine wire wool until you are certain it is all removed. Wipe with a cloth and white spirit to check for any last traces—if the cloth is discoloured, something is still on the wood. If you have bought a piece of stripped pine furniture, it will probably have wax on it and this will need removing before staining or other finishing is possible.

French Polish (shellac): If your work piece is solid wood (not veneer) you can use methylated spirit and fine wire wool to remove the polish. Methylated spirit contains water and raises the grain of the wood, giving you extra work sanding it smooth later. If you do strip polish with methylated spirits, be careful not to soak any veneer, inlays or marquetry.

The alternative is to use a

white-spirit-soluble liquid paint stripper (buy one that states it will remove polish) and fine wire wool.

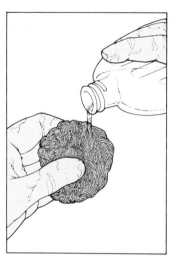

Apply the stripper to the wire wool and, when this becomes clogged with polish, put it into a metal container and start another.

Work quickly on veneer as the stripper could soften the glue that holds it down. As each small area is stripped, clean immediately with white spirit on a cloth. Don't leave the stripper on the wood as if you were stripping paint.

Varnish and Cellulose Lacquer: These should be stripped with a liquid stripper as for paint; but you shouldn't need as much stripper and it should take less time to work. Use a stripper that states it will remove cellulose lacquer. Clean with white spirit to remove all trace of stripper.

If the piece is veneered, try using wire wool as described above.

This old varnished scullery dresser was purchased at a very reasonable cost because of its rather lacklustre, dark appearance. After stripping and refinishing, while not perfect, it becomes an attractive addition to any kitchen. New fittings help to enhance its bright, fresh appearance. A piece of furniture this size takes some time to strip, so it would be best to house it in a garage or little used room until finished.

Sanding and Filling

Sanding

Now that the wood is bare, you can assess the condition of the surface. Check carefully for dents, scratches and burns.

Shallow scratches can be sanded out, but too much sanding in one place can leave a depression that will be noticeable later. While sanding, try to widen the area around a scratch to blend with the surface. Always sand in the direction of the grain—never across it.

An electric orbital (not a disc) sander is useful for large flat surfaces, but use a fine grit paper as there will be small circular scratches that will need sanding by hand in the direction of the grain. If possible, use these machines outside as they create a lot of dust, and wear goggles and face mask.

For flat surfaces, the sandpaper should be wrapped around a block of wood, or a cork or rubber sanding block.

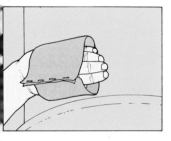

When dealing with large curves, you can staple the two ends of the paper together and put your hand through the middle, like a glove. For grooves and awkward shapes, wrap the paper around any object that will give you a useful shape. The important thing is to sand all the wood thoroughly. Be careful with veneer—it's possible to sand right through it, especially near the edges.

Dents can sometimes be pulled up again if you place a damp cloth over them and warm them with a domestic iron. Once again, this treatment is not suitable for veneer.

Burns must be sanded out until the charred colour is removed, and filled if necessary.

Filling

Before filling, decide whether you wish to change the colour of the wood (and perhaps test a small area) so you know what colour of filler to use. In general, fillers should be a little darker than the final colour of the wood as they won't absorb stain once they're dry.

If the wood will not have heavy wear, a little *wax* (from a crayon or candle of a suitable colour) melted in a spoon and dripped into the fault will do. Let the wax cool and gently shave off the excess with a sharp blade.

If you intend to varnish the piece, you will need to seal all the wax repairs with a shellac polish first, as oil-based products will not adhere to the wax.

Alternatively, use a cigarette lighter to melt a *shellac stick* of an appropriate colour over the fault and, when it begins to harden, use a sharp blade to remove the excess. Rub smooth with fine wire wool.

For more durable fillers, use *proprietary stopper*. These come in various colours and shades that can be mixed together or with woodstains.

Apply the stopper with a flexible knife, leave until hard, then sand smooth. Try to keep the filler from spreading away from the dent. It tends to show in the grain of the surrounding wood if rubbed in when it's wet. It is better to overfill and sand off later than to spread it around.

Remember that you can't restore any surface to perfection, so it's worth considering how much filling your furniture really needs. A slight dent in the surface is preferable to a large expanse of filler.

Grain filler is used to fill the pores on open grain hardwoods such as mahogany, oak, ash and beech. The pores appear as tiny pinholes or as lines in the surface and they will show in the finish.

The easiest way to fill them is to use proprietary grain filler that is applied by brush or cloth. When partially dry, it is rubbed off across the grain, leaving the filler only in the grain and not on the surface. When completely dry, it should be sanded smooth. More than one application may be necessary.

Changing the Colour

Now that you have prepared the bare wood, you have the choice of staining it darker or bleaching it lighter. If the wood has accidental stains that still show after stripping and sanding, you can try a two-part wood bleach over the whole surface. This should remove the stains, but will lighten the wood as well. If desired, it can then be stained darker again.

Bleaching is best done with proprietary wood bleach systems and the manufacturers' instructions should be followed exactly. One point to remember is that all bleaches require the use of water, so you are advised not to use them on veneers.

Stains are available in three types—oil-, spirit-, and water-based. The easiest to use are oil-based as they do not raise the grain or affect veneer. Choose one that states it is diluted with white spirit and buy colours from one manufacturer to be sure you can mix them together to get the colour you want. Test on an inconspicuous part of the piece in strong daylight. Apply the stain with a soft lint-free cloth (or a brush can be used for large areas). Try not to flood the surface of the wood and keep working until each surface is evenly covered. Overlapping where stain has already penetrated will produce a dark line. You

Stripped and stained to resemble mahogany, this desk, shelf and window frame have been brought together to make an attractive work area.

Right: *Here is a selection from the extensive range of colours and natural wood shades widely available in stains and varnishes.*

should also watch out for areas of wood that are more absorbent than the rest, especially ends of pieces of wood (end grain) and edges near joints. Wiping with white spirit before staining will help to make the absorbency more constant. Subsequent coats of stain will darken the wood further, but as it is not removable, test an inconspicuous area beforehand. Stains work best with natural wood colours. Results may be disappointing with other colours such as green, blue, etc. because of the different areas of absorbency in the wood. For these colours, it is better to use coloured varnish.

Coloured varnish is available in various colours and natural wood shades as well as matt, satin, and gloss finish. There is the advantage of applying both colour and finish in one operation, but as the colour is on the surface, any chipping will show the bare wood colour beneath. In order to keep the colour even, it is best to apply a coat of clear varnish before the coloured one. This will keep areas of greater absorbency from showing darker.

Fuming is another way of darkening wood. It is suitable for hardwoods such as oak, mahogany and walnut. See page 30 for the technique.

Refinishing

The range of finishes for wood is extremely wide, but in choosing one, bear in mind the wear the surface will receive. For instance, coloured varnish on a door or door frame would soon be chipped, and French polish on a kitchen table would be spoiled with normal use. So, first decide whether the surface should be heat, water and alcohol proof.

Traditional oil, wax, and shellac-based polish finishes are marred or stained by hot plates, water and spilled drinks, and general hard wear. Therefore, table tops, work surfaces, banisters, doors, chairs, etc. are best finished with polyurethane sealer, polyurethane varnish, or two-part plastic resin finishes. These will stand up well and may be waxed to mellow their appearance. On the other hand, some furniture and many parts of woodwork receive very little wear and aren't threatened by heat or liquids. With these you have the choice of any finish.

Here is a list of finishing methods, starting with the two types that are easiest to apply and give the best results.

Sealers and polyurethane varnish

(hard wearing, heat and moisture proof)
A sealer differs from a varnish in that it is absorbed into the surface of the wood rather than forming a film on top of it.

However, for furniture (as opposed to floors) two coats of matt-finish varnish thinned 10% with white spirit is an effective sealer. It will protect the wood from liquids and dirt, while avoiding the slightly artificial look of several coats of gloss

varnish. It is also easier to apply as it is brushed on thinly and each coat (including the final one) is lightly rubbed with fine wire wool to remove any runs or rough spots.

When the final coat is dry, you should apply several coats of wax polish to protect it. Maintenance is simply an occasional wipe and coat of polish.

Shellac-based polishes

(easy and quick to apply; neither hard wearing nor heat proof)
There are several of these, namely French polish, button polish, white sealer, etc. They are all easy to apply as wood sealers and have the advantage of drying very quickly.

Apply them by brush or cloth, thinning with methylated

spirits if necessary. Rub down lightly with fine wire wool between coats. As they dry so quickly, there shouldn't be any waiting. Apply successive coats until the surface of the wood seems full and smooth. Allow the final coat to dry for a few hours and then apply several coats of wax polish.

This finish should not be confused with traditional French polishing.

Traditional wax finish

(hard work; neither hard wearing nor heat proof)
Melt equal quantities of shredded beeswax and turpentine in a tin placed in a dish of hot water. The vapour is inflammable so don't do this near a flame. Once melted, stir and allow to cool.

Far left: *These new handles and fittings are in keeping with the style of the piece. The blanket method of stripping would be useful for the carvings on the back.*

Left: *The windows have been painted white to match the rough plaster walls and lace edged blinds, while the surrounds have been stripped and stained to match the table and chairs.*

Apply a thin coat with a cloth, rubbing in a circular motion to work the wax well into the grain. Leave it for 24 hours to harden, and then polish vigorously. At least 5 coats will be necessary.

Modern wax finish

There are several proprietary wax polishes that are faster drying and more resilient than beeswax. These come with full instructions but remember that wax on bare wood is not a very practical finish. You can always seal first with shellac or polyurethane varnish.

Traditional oil finish

(*hard work; not heat proof*)
Mix equal parts of boiled and raw linseed oil and simmer for 15 minutes. Add $\frac{1}{8}$th part

turpentine, and allow to cool.

Rub the oil into the wood with 400 grit wet and dry paper, working with the grain. Wipe off the slurry that is produced with a cloth, rubbing across the grain, and leave to dry for 24 hours. Repeat until a shiny finish is produced.

Cloths used with this oil should be disposed of by burning immediately after use as there is a danger of spontaneous combustion.

Modern oil finish

(*easy; not heat proof*)
Teak oil or Danish oil do not produce the high gloss of the traditional oil finish, but they can be reapplied easily and can be buffed to a satin sheen.

Apply with brush or cloth and allow to dry. Read the

instructions on the tin as some products contain fungicide and are meant for outdoor use only.

Cloths should be disposed of by burning immediately after use as there is a danger of spontaneous combustion.

Polyurethane varnish

This is the most popular do-it-yourself finish, available in gloss, satin, and matt finishes. Apply with a soft brush, the first coat thinned 10% with white spirit. At least two coats will be needed. Rub down with fine steel wool between each. Mellow the last coat with wax polish.

Some modern varnishes come in microporous form. These are ideal on wood that may be damp, for they let the moisture escape through their porous surface.

FLOORS

Wooden floors are of two kinds. The most common are *floorboards* (usually softwood, but not always) that are nailed to timbers beneath. The other type is *hardwood block, strip* or *parquet*. These consist of pieces of hardwood that are glued to a smooth surface below. Some modern floors of this type use veneered plywood, rather than solid wood; these are not suitable for stripping. It is only in preparation that the two types are treated differently.

Sanding and sealing of floors must be done in one operation, so you must arrange to have all the materials beforehand and allow plenty of time without traffic in the room. The room should be emptied of all furnishings.

The size of the room will determine the amount of time required, but it is important not to mark the floor once it has been sanded, and also to apply the coats of sealer in quick succession—i.e. as soon as the previous coat is dry, but before it sets hard.

If circumstances make it necessary to leave the job for a day between coats, it will be necessary to rub the sealed floor with wire wool to 'key' the next coat. If there is to be a planned stop overnight, it would be better to stop after the sanding and apply the first coat of sealer the next day.

Drying time may vary between products, so plan your schedule according to the manufacturers' recommendations.

Parquet – hardwood blocks laid, in this instance, in a herringbone pattern.

Floorboards – the softwood planks in this childrens room are in excellent condition.

Sanding and Staining Floors

Materials: Belt floor sander; rotary disc floor sander for the edges and corners; vacuum cleaner; paint brush (preferably a little narrower than the floorboards); wood stain (optional); proprietary floor seal; fine wire wool; rubber gloves; rags; electric floor polisher (optional); goggles to protect your eyes; face mask to avoid inhaling dust particles.

Preparation

Floorboards. Pull out all carpet tacks and nail down loose boards.

Woodblock and parquet. Pull out all carpet tacks and check for loose pieces.

Clean any dust and debris out of the holes until the loose pieces fit flush with the others.

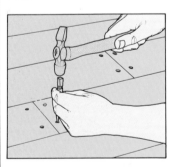

Using a nail punch, drive all nail heads down at least 3mm below the surface. Be sure not to miss any as they could damage the sanding machine.

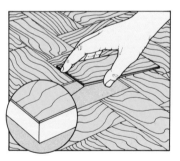

Pull up and check a piece of your parquet floor to make sure it's solid wood. Veneered plywood (as illustrated above) is not suitable for sanding.

Glue down any loose pieces with contact adhesive. If there is a large build up of wax on the floor, remove most of it with wire wool and white spirit.

The two types of sander you need are widely available for hire, and should come with plenty of replacement sanding belts and discs on a 'pay for what you use' basis. If possible, hire a sander of the vacuum type which cleans up most of the dust created by the sanding. There is more of this than you probably imagine. It is advisable to completely close the room to contain the dust.

Commence work with the belt sander, using a medium grit belt. Remember that if you are sanding softwood floorboards you will be removing more wood from the surface than if the floor is hardwood block or parquet.

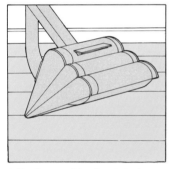

Tilt the machine back before switching on—**'never allow the sander to run on the spot'** as it will sand a deep furrow into the floor.

Once the machine is running, lower the belt gently as you move off diagonally across the floor. At the end of the strip, tilt the machine back before you stop and turn around for the next strip.

The speed you move across the floor determines the depth of cut, so proceed smoothly and steadily, sanding as much of the floor as possible with the large sander. Remove only as much wood as necessary.

Next, use a medium grit disc on the rotary sander to sand the edges and places where the belt sander wouldn't reach. The last corners can be rubbed down by hand with sandpaper wrapped around a block, rubbing with the grain.

Always wear goggles and face mask.

Don't wear loose clothing or ties.

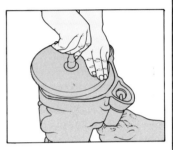

Change the disc on the rotary sander to fine grit and go around all the edges and corners again. This is to smooth the surface of the wood, so try to work in the direction of the grain (except on parquet). Be sure to cover all the areas you previously sanded with the rotary sander. Doing the edges at this stage means there will be less walking on the main part of the floor after its final sanding.

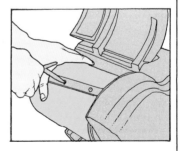

Now, change the belt on the large sander to fine grit and smooth the main part of the

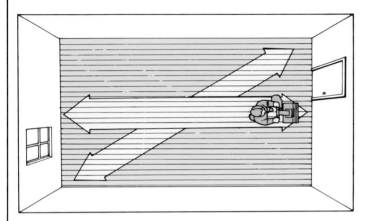

Apply the stain evenly with a lint-free cloth. Rubber gloves will keep the stain from your fingers. Do a small area at a time, working continuously in one direction. Dealing with the entire length of one or two boards at once is a good idea. Try not to overlap areas already stained or there will be a dark edge. Allow to dry thoroughly before applying seal.

floor. This time, work along the length of the boards—i.e. with the grain—not diagonally as before.

Vacuum the entire room thoroughly to remove all dust—the worst enemy of a good finish is wood dust, so take the sanders out of the room and don't forget to clean the tops of skirting boards etc. A cloth dampened with white spirit will pick up the last traces from the floor.

Staining

If you want to stain the wood darker, now is the time to do it.

These pieces of softwood (of the type usually found as floorboards) show how stain or coloured varnish can subdue or bring out the grain. Test a small area first.

Sealing Floors

Following sanding (and any staining) a floor is completely 'bare' and must be sealed. The purpose of sealer is to soak into the wood and so prevent liquids and dirt from being absorbed or moisture from evaporating.

Sealer should not be confused with varnish, which is a finish (similar to paint) and not practical for floors as it will eventually crack and chip. The floor will then need re-sanding and refinishing. It is better to use a proprietary floor seal, such as urea-formaldehyde. This is not as brittle and needs only an occasional coat of wax for protection.

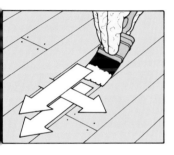

Floorboards. Brush the sealer on liberally, working along one or two boards, first with the grain, then across it to spread it evenly, and finally lightly with the grain again to minimize brush marks.

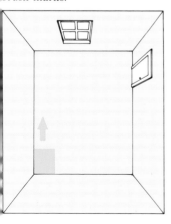

Parquet. Start in the furthest corner from the door and work quickly. Work in sections of about 1 metre square, and try to finish each strip before the seal dries.

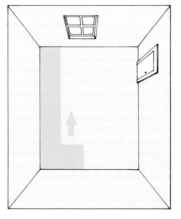

As one strip is finished, go back to the other end of it to start the next strip. That way the seal will have as little time as possible to dry along the edge and cause a visible overlap with the next strip.

As the seal dries, you will be able to see where the wood is still absorbent. When the first coat is dry, but before it hardens (see the manufacturers' instructions), apply the second coat. For parquet and woodblock floors, divide the area into different strips from the first coat to keep the overlaps from building up.

When this coat is dry, judge whether the wood is well sealed or requires further coats. Hardwood parquet, block and strip floors will be less absorbent than softwood floorboards and so will require fewer coats. Two coats should be enough for hardwood.

When the final coat is dry, feel around the surface for any rough patches where the grain of the wood may feel 'furry'. Rub these with fine wire wool to smooth them before the seal sets hard. Remove the dust immediately, and leave the seal to harden.

Furniture or traffic will mark the floor during this time. The manufacturers' instructions will state how long it must be left.

Polishing
After it has fully cured (hardened), the surface must be protected with several coats of silicone wax polish.

Many types of floor polish are available, including glossy, matt and non-slip. The more coats, the better the finish and protection, so don't skimp.

Apply the polish according to the instructions. An electric floor polisher is useful for this first polishing, though it's up to you to decide whether to hire or buy one.

Maintenance
The floor is now protected against spills and scuffing, and should need only a quick buff with a cloth (or electric polisher) to keep the shine in the most used areas.

Stubborn stains will come off if you wipe them with white spirit or one of the cleaner/polishes that are available.

SPECIAL EFFECTS

Furniture, floors and woodwork can be personalized still further with wood stain or paint applied either freehand or by stencilling. The traditional paint used was buttermilk with pigment added to produce soft earth colours. This effect can easily be achieved today with modern emulsion or acrylic paints, but remember that, on wood, soft colours look best. **Paint** is easier to use than stain as it is applied after the wood has been sealed and mistakes are easily wiped off while wet.

The best way to begin is to buy ready-cut stencil plates from craft and art shops. You should also use the brushes made for the purpose. These are round with the bristles trimmed flat and are held vertically to stipple the paint through the plate. This helps prevent the paint from creeping under the edges of the plate and spoiling the design. The best paints to use are artists' acrylic-based colours, sold in tubes by art shops. They have the advantage of being quick drying and having a consistency that covers well in one coat.

On floors or other places likely to receive hard wear, the finished stencil should have seal or varnish applied over it to protect it. **Stains** must be used on bare wood and the result is permanent. Also they can only be used to darken, not lighten, a surface. However, if the design isn't too ambitious, delicate effects that are very hard wearing can be created.

Interest is added to this stripped pine corner display cabinet by painting the inside with matt finish oil-based paint.

Before laying, pieces of this beautiful oak floor were stained black to achieve this pattern. This was a demanding task as any mistakes made with stain are permanent.

Discreet touches of colour enhance the design of this unusual bedside cupboard.

How to Stencil

Stencilling with paint

Wood must be sealed beforehand, but remove any wax with white spirit.

Tools and materials: Stencil plate; stencil brushes; tubes of acrylic paint; masking tape; a board or something to use as a 'dabbing board' or palette; newspapers; a piece of chalk; cloth to wipe up excess or spilled paint.

Stencilling with stains

As this must be done on the bare wood, take every precaution against getting stain where it's not wanted. If you're working on the floor, protect it with dust sheets (not newspapers) to avoid marks caused by walking on it.

Setting out the design and fixing the stencil plates is the same as for paint.

Use a cloth to apply the stain, rather than a brush. The danger is that the stain will creep under the edges of the plate as it is absorbed into the wood.

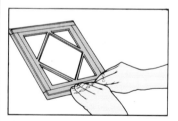

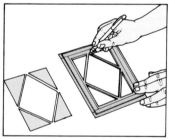

Measure and lay out the design, lightly marking with chalk the positions in which you will place the plate. Tape the plate into position and ensure it is flat against the surface.

Squeeze some paint on to the palette and dab the brush in it; then, dab it on newspaper until it leaves an even circle of paint. This is the correct amount of paint to hold in the brush.

With the same dabbing motion, apply the paint through the holes in the plate. Repeat with any other holes and other colours needed to complete the part of the design covered by the plate in this position. Use a different brush for each colour. Remove the plate very carefully to avoid smudging the design, and wipe it clean before re-positioning it.

It may help to trace the outline of the design with a felt tip pen in a suitable colour before staining. This also helps to give more definition to the edges.

After staining, the wood must be finished as described earlier. If you are using varnish or seal, use a minimum of brushing—the solvent may smear the stain.

Ready cut stencil plates in a wide range of designs are available from art shops.

TOP TEN TIPS

1 Start small! Try stripping a small box or chair before tackling a large project.

2 Repair the furniture before stripping it rather than afterwards. That way you'll have a better idea of how the repair will look when it's refinished, and also the glue and dirty hand marks won't be absorbed by the bare wood.

Drawers that don't close properly are a common problem and the fault is usually worn runners. You must either add just enough wood to the runners (or the bottom of the drawer) for it to close straight and sit squarely in its opening, or replace the runners with new ones.

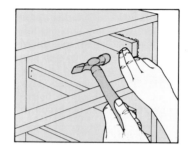

To replace runners, mark a straight line where they should be and glue and pin new strips. Make sure the edges of the drawer that sit on the runners are straight as they may be worn too.

Metal plates and *angle brackets* that can be used to strengthen furniture and woodwork are widely available.

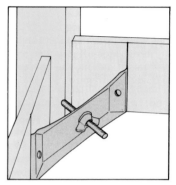

This corner bracket for table legs takes some effort to fit, but is very strong. It uses a bolt screwed diagonally into the leg and a plate which is fixed to the underframe of the table. A nut then pulls the bolt (and the leg) tightly into the corner of the underframe.

Fuming

Fuming is a traditional way of darkening hardwoods such as oak, mahogany and walnut. In a suitable, well ventilated work area, such as outdoors or in a garage, where the flooring material will not be damaged, make a tent with a sheet of polythene. Stand the piece to be treated inside the tent with an open dish of .880 ammonia (specially formulated for this purpose and available from some paint suppliers and chemists). Place weights around the edges to make the tent as airtight as possible and leave it for an hour or so. To check for colour change, rub an unseen area with a cloth dipped in linseed oil. The longer the wood is fumed, the darker it will be. Warning – ammonia fumes are poisonous, so take care not to inhale them.

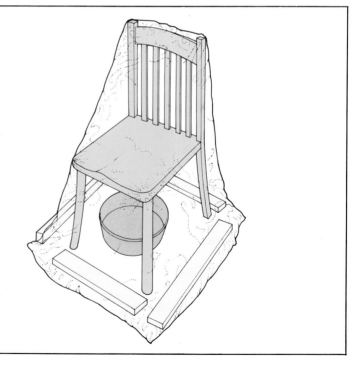

Loose or creaking stair treads can be cured by fixing metal shelf brackets underneath to stop the movement—providing the underside of the stairs is accessible.

3 Metal fittings should be removed before you strip any wood. Handles, catches and locks that are broken will need to be replaced. When shopping for new ones, take an old fitting with you so you can get one of the correct size. In the case of handles, make sure the new ones will cover the fixing holes of the old, but don't fit them until the job is complete.

4 Try to use the least drastic method for stripping wood. Liquid and jellied strippers (especially those that wash off with white spirit rather than water) are less hard on wood than the caustic pastes that must be removed with water. *Never* use water on veneer.

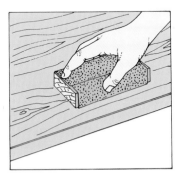

5 A good finish depends on the smoothness of the wood. Sand all surfaces with fine grade abrasive paper in the direction of the grain. When sanding veneer, be careful not to sand through it, especially along edges.

6 Use a dry paintbrush (or a brush attachment on a vacuum cleaner) to remove all dust from the grain of the wood after sanding. Then use a cloth dampened with white spirit to pick up any last traces before applying the finish.

7 Furniture that is sold already stripped will probably have wax on it. Before refinishing, you will have to remove the wax with white spirit and fine wire wool.

8 Always test the colour of stain or finish on an unseen part of the wood.

9 To prevent stain from appearing darker where the wood is more absorbent, wipe the surface with white spirit and then with a dry cloth just before applying the stain.

10 Hard finishes such as polyurethane varnish, sealer, and French polish take several days to cure (harden) after they dry. Don't put objects on shelves, window sills, and floors too soon or the finish will be marked.

Safety Tips

Protect everything (including your skin) from contact with chemical strippers. Wear rubber gloves and old clothes and, if possible, do the job outside.

Stripping products are poisonous. Read all safety warnings about first aid *before* it becomes necessary to take action.

Never store chemicals in bottles or jars that could be mistaken by children for soft drinks etc. Always label clearly and store away from children and animals.

Some chemical strippers can dissolve plastic buckets etc. Always use a metal container for disposing of the residue.

Rags used to apply oil to wood are a serious fire risk. Always dispose of them immediately after use by burning.

Shellac polishes can burn at very low temperatures. Store them in small, airtight containers and don't use them near naked lights.

Always wear goggles and a mask when using mechanical sanders.

Don't wear loose clothing or ties while using power tools.

Useful Addresses

Australia
Timber Development
 Association (NSW) Pty Ltd,
 Sydney, NSW.
Timber Promotion Council of
 Victoria, Blackburn, Victoria.
Timber Research and
 Development advisory
 Council, Newstead,
 Queensland, and Cairns,
 Queensland.
Timber Development
 Association of South
 Australia, Kent Town, S.A.
Forest Products Association of
 West Australia, West Perth,
 W.A.

Britain
Timber Research and
 Development Association,
 High Wycombe, Bucks HP14
 4ND.

Canada
Canadian Wood Council,
 Ottawa, Ontario, K1P 6A4.

New Zealand
New Zealand Forest Service,
 Wellington.

South Africa
Timber and Allied Trades
 Association, Johannesburg.

Author
Dek Messecar
Series Consultant Editor
Bob Tattersall
Design
Mike Rose and Bob Lamb
Picture Research
Ann Lyons
Illustrations
Rob Shone

Dek Messecar is a professional joiner who has had experience of
all aspects of DIY.

Bob Tattersall has been a DIY journalist for over 25 years and was
editor of *Homemaker* for 16 years. He now works as a freelance
journalist and broadcaster. Regular contact with the main DIY
manufacturers keeps him up-to-date on all new products and
developments. He has written many books on various aspects of
DIY and, while he is considered 'an expert', he prefers to think of
himself as a do-it-yourselfer who happens to be a journalist.

Photographs from Elizabeth Whiting Photo Library, except for pages
6 and 7, courtesy of Timber Research and Development Association;
page 17, courtesy of Sikkens UK Ltd; page 24, courtesy of Blackfriars
Paints, Bristol

Cover photography by Carl Warner

The *Do It! Series* was conceived, edited and designed by Elizabeth
Whiting & Associates and Robert Lamb & Company for William
Collins Sons and Co Ltd

© 1983 Elizabeth Whiting & Associates and Robert Lamb &
Company

First published 1983
Reprinted 1983, 1985, 1986, 1987 (twice)

Revised edition first published 1989
9 8 7 6 5 4 3 2 1

Published by William Collins Sons & Co Ltd
London · Glasgow · Sydney · Auckland
Toronto · Johannesburg

ISBN 0 00 411893 6

Printed in Spain